AF344686

aw, tits!

Tiana Kirk

BookLeaf Publishing

India | USA | UK

aw, tits! © 2024 Tiana Kirk

All rights reserved.

No part of this publication may be reproduced, stored in a retrieval system, or transmitted, in any form or by any means, electronic, mechanical, photocopying, recording or otherwise, without the prior written permission of the presenters.

Tiana Kirk asserts the moral right to be identified as author of this work.

Presentation by *BookLeaf Publishing*

Web: www.bookleafpub.com

E-mail: info@bookleafpub.com

First edition 2024

for the ones I fear I'll lose the most - not because of something I could do, but because of something I could never be

ACKNOWLEDGEMENT

For everyone that I asked: "Would it be annoying if I wrote another book?"
I have infinite affection, respect, and trust for you and the volume of which you demanded my follow through of the idea

PREFACE

There is something so deeply unserious about being twenty-seven.

There is nothing groundbreaking or glass-ceiling shattering to be read here about it though.
I am sitting in an unbroken room, uncomfortably, with my peers, blind to my accomplishments that are piled neatly around me like bricks in a round tower.

I love people who do not love me back the way I deserve.
I move away from people who want me to stay.
I ache for the innocence of childhood laughter
and yearn for faster moving clocks to allow more progress to be made.

I allow my inept internal compass to guide me, hoping the confidence and trust will fix it one day
and I'll be able to look back and laugh.

In these foolish times of mid-twenties crises, when mirrors and memories become distorted one can fight to swim against the current or allow oneself to be swept away and enjoy the view.

If one opts in for the anticipation of the unknown
rather than the exhaustive attempts to return to what once was,
there is nothing else to do but shrug, smile, and exclaim: "aw, tits!"

is this all worth it?

acrylic nails that counteract my height
make me feel feminine and slight
painted my favourite colour
that prevent me from playing guitar
the fancy degree parchment
that feels decorative, though it pays my rent
the animal companions that will forever be
out of reach much sooner than I can accept
the house full of accolades, memories,
impending dread of moving all of the shit out of
the storage rooms.

In a hypothetical, if I could go back and
have a re-do scenario,
get placed in my seven-year-old body,
only knowing how things would turn out
twenty years down the road
would I believe that all I have now
is it worth going through all I would have to
re-endure just to get…here?

I'm so afraid I know the answer could change
tomorrow's version versus yesterday's
it's felt so stagnant and stale as of late
I don't believe I'd choose to go through it again

there's nowhere to place that blame
the daily choices are inconsequential
they all have shades of worse or better
but I've been sitting in a canyon and wonder
if I'll never be able to leave, or if another
is just past the next crest
and if the timing of it all
is the only thing in that hypothetical
that actually matters.

did I turn the stove off?

I'm up too late again tonight
- this morning, if I'm being annoying
senselessly scrolling through years of sleep aid
videos
to find the last one you put on for me

I'm on our couch, that was always mine
but you'd sat beside me on it
stroked my back and hair
when your right hand was free, in between
playing games
on our switch that was always yours

we were really good in that way
the melding into "ours" made easy
maybe that's why it's so hard now to

unmeld

why it's still comforting
not as often but just as deeply
to replay memories of being loved by you
to save the brief, palpable, melt-into-you
moments for emotionally rainy days

in an armoured safe with a passcode we'd both
know, tattooing it just in case

the ones of loving you remain
on the back burner in a simmer pot
always filling the room so sweetly
always threatening to evaporate completely
if I forget to put the lid back on

if I use my insomnia to my advantage
hallucinate the memories in a lucid state
you're still there, across the field
catching and tossing the same old ball around
in our hand-me-down mitts
smiling at the scent: sawdust, varnish, and sweat
the combination couldn't dream of being so
romantic

had me feeling like forever in its infancy
holding hands with you
one foot in Hades' pool
the other in the fountain of youth
in a state of perpetual agelessness

as long as I don't move an inch or blink
we're still there

but winds whisper, clouds shift, without
permission or intent

the face I thought I saw on the wall
was merely a smudge, a reminder
I've fallen behind on housework

one day soon, I'm sure
I won't be able to recognize you, could hurt
or maybe I'll have healed by then
guess I won't know until I do

if the same gray-blue eyes that could speak
to me will have long lost all fluency
to inside jokes and winding roads we'd dreamed
of getting lost down happily

I'd like to hope you didn't know the extent
and pace of your falling out of love
until it was too late to pull the rope
or reach out to hands you'd grown tired of

years or mere days from now
our eyes will meet
and catch a flicker of the people we used to be
together
and for the briefest of moments
we'll nod, smile, and know
that the kids in love we left behind
are a stone safely stowed
and best left unturned, undisturbed,
on the furthest back burner in our minds

out with the old, in with you

I've been so lucky to love so deeply
forming such long-lasting connections
unbreakable bonds - at the time

I've been so lonely when love is unseeded
foraging, seeking, longing for affection
heart breakable by my hand at any time

by that, I suppose I'm speculating
to think that maybe you feel luckier, too,
than average-hearted folk
seasons have passed by a time or two
I think maybe I'm not as lucky as I thought
or my heart is smaller broke

did you take it from me
or did I give it freely
because I felt bad for how you were hurting
and felt bad from how you'd hurt me?

I don't blame you, and I won't name you
in a room of people I've loved
as the most, one day, I swear

maybe by then, associations

will have a use and
muscle memory dementia
will have loosened
the knots in the emotional Palomar
you tied while twiddling your thumbs

----

when it comes to the past
- loves I know I'll always have
and never again hold
I know they're not wasted effort,
time, or most of all love,
- the mosaic gold
all the micro tears and abrasions,
my woes, the errs in judgment
and my abundant impatience
led me down the cliched path
that had no meaning until you took my hand

I'd never felt the type of desired
the kind of pined over, resign your life over
to the kind of forever you believe in
that I do every time our eyes meet

I don't know if I'll understand just what it was
that made you the man that knew he needed me
but I'd be sitting pretty if and when I got the
chance
to sit by your handsome side in silence
and get to untie each other's knotted pasts

thinkingitoverthinkingitovert hinkingit

obstinately yearning
because you're not? because it's enough for me?
because the pain fuels my writing? because the
chase feels like exercising?
is my baggage so much heavier than yours or
more awkward to carry?

are you oh so inspirational or am I bored,
blurry-eyed, and sick of loving you off the
record?
are you just tall and well-endowed,
and the funniest person I'll ever know?

have I actually loved you through this vernal
drought?
save all this questioning, I've no reason to doubt
I don't love you any less or feel differently
whether you're ignoring or inside me

is this pain I've been through enough to
convince you?

maybe you'd be able and more willing to look
into my eyes when we speak

if you weren't just as trapped in this - does it
make any difference?

analytical spelunker

I don't think you could say honestly
what I could've done differently
you might just land on "trying harder" or
"staying"

it's heartbreaking that my best
wasn't better or more evident
because I tried my hardest to stay

through all your emotional turbulence
you pushed and shoved me away
and got upset I became distant

treated me like I was putting on an act
or doling out a punishment

neither of us were treated fairly
by the other's perceived uncaring
but how can I be the only one who sees
all the love we could be sharing

while you listen to your sad boy music
affirming how deserving and worthy you are
of the love you're locking out

against my requests, my family still asks
about you and your life as if I know

the months drag by
you haven't changed anything
but your mind about wanting me
and that feels like enough to keep me reeling
still stalking my socials, pretending you're fine
faking it til you make me crazy

you were never any good at
a serious conversation between us
without pitching a fit or a tent in the process

is that your intent?
are you just indifferent?
are you any different?

recent daydreams I

an inhumane reality
no one lives here, save me
I walk down the stairs
and feel you meet me half there
touch the door at the same time
swear I can see you outside

but
      it's
          only
                ever
                    me

can't bring myself to sigh
and make the daydream sleepwalk fantasies
any more a part of the real world

nothing so pathetic deserves
to live such a cruel existence
so I keep it to myself and wonder
if this is what manifestation is

conjuring entire scenarios
where we are hanging out with broken bones
just so you'll pay a touch more attention to me

while vividly and viciously recalling how you
used to spread my thighs only with your knees

my double bed has never felt more empty

my body is still pretending
only one side of it exists or belongs to it
it was christened and cherished entirely by me
no hand-me-downs stained by hurt feelings
I was still healing

for over a year I'd slept indecisively
flirting with any side that'd have me
but I'm unhappily married to the left side
have claimed my territory
the indent of my body becoming less slight
each night I stubbornly lay here, sorry

the open window's behind me
and if you were beside me
you'd have the last laugh
while the too-cool summer air wafts
against my exposed skin, brazenly
ruining the potential for even mediocre sleep

so maybe I stay to be taken away
in an eventual dream to recall
what it felt like to past-me
switching sides while asleep

waking up with your arms
wrapped around my body pseudo-apologetically
all to be forgiven
with morning breath kisses
and a healthy sense of wry wit
"if I wanted my spot, I should've fought for it"
spoken so casually
as though my knuckles weren't deeply violet

flip

please don't come back
if you've made your choice
even if it's wrong
your regrets are none of my business anymore

it wouldn't feel as hypocritical
coming from my mouth
if you'd been the first to the punch
but go on, my love, keep playing dumb
you're only fooling everyone else
weaponizing my intelligence
I should've given up but now I'm stuck

mistakes I make, steps I take
to try my best to be the best to you and I
are never met with more than apologetic texts
and stifled laughter from my friends
who can't wait to witness this puppy love
get euthanized

flop

you could come over if you wanted to
I know you know, but I'd like you to, y'know?

not say a thing, just hold tight to me
and be sad together in the same part of the city
instead of holding fast to these thirty-odd
kilometres
that only exist between us because you wanted
to get closer

the irony is not lost on me

do you miss me like I do?
it doesn't matter really, not to anyone but me
and I guess that's why I'm asking my notes app
and not you

I thought everything was pointless without me
Do you hate yourself for all the missed
opportunities?

two years ago I was in another country,
months from even learning of your existence
playing games, indifferent

last year you were mine, officially
I told you I loved you when you kissed me at my
door
but I knew it was days, maybe weeks before

the wasted potential is devastating
but I guess it goes without saying
it's my fault we never made it to today
to celebrate what could've been

it is what it is and
I wish you all the happiness
but by that I mean
I hope you learn to find it intrinsically

I don't miss begging you to stop being mean,
to stop exploiting all my boundaries
but I cherish our laughter deeply
the way you smell and sound and feel me

it's not my fault you wouldn't go to therapy
and it wasn't me that made you need it
I wasn't bluffing, I said I'd leave
I never lied when I owed you honesty

friends

we can still be friends
if we promise to never lie
we can be friends, still
we never bother making time
can we be still, friends
ask me if I've lost my mind

we were never really friends
when we weren't under the tightly gripped
umbrella contexts of our inclement relationship

I give you space and time from me loving you
you volunteer to give me a ride to the hospital
I feel bad for hurting you and still wanting you
back
you feel bad that you fucked me while knowing
that

I'm not going to ask if that's why you still reply
to my texts
maybe it's enough to get some semblance of rest
to know you'll eventually be around for the
less-than-best of times
I'll let you in on the priceless secrets you'll treat
like dimes

but we can still be friends, right?

self-destructive tendencies

you ask me how I am,
I say, "I'll live," and
probably will until I'm too old
to remember who I am
or how I got love-conned into
this less fun kind of chokehold

not so long ago
you'd asked to sit in, fully clothed
and watch while I bathed
upstairs in your parents' home

every invitation was accepted
before the offer had fully left my lips
so eager, you pounced on them as if
you knew they'd one day not exist
but I'm still here, sending signals
no longer mixed

you've caged your yeses in your
jail cell mouth until you bleed for show
like you're tryna win a contest of
who's the more stubborn Scorpio

it's not impressive,

I'm guessing it's easy to go a day
without thinking of me
but once the night hits,
I'd be surprised if
you'd never begged to forget me
and the way
my fingers can graze
all the right places
or the heat of my breath on your neck
and the old standby - your hands capsized
advertent and precisely determined
to play hide and seek between my thighs

I wish you didn't need to be alone
as much as I needed not to
I wish you'd just listen
and give me a minute
to tell you with my hands
how much I've been missing you

I wouldn't say a thing
you didn't want to hear
though it wouldn't go
over silently
no conversation could be
constructed in dreams
that would suit both our needs
so violently

recent daydreams II

peering out the kitchen window
hoping to catch a glimpse of you
I know it's pathetic but I can't regret it
won't betray my memory of
your pattern-esque parking habits
when you wanted to be seen

I live for the blind hope of it all
only when I know it's less than
likely to go my way
I've no idea how I managed to re-fall
just as you were starting to walk away

it's like my heart's been asleep,
and the pins and needles creep
through my veins with every step I take
each day I see something new from our history
I'm stuck in a bubble, living in a memory
confused and terrified as to why
the stabbing sensation won't set me free

that heart-shaped rock we found about a year
ago
sits nice and quiet in my bag everywhere I go
reminds me the love was real

even if it's not really there anymore

the more I know
the more I hurt my own feelings
so I sit in the dark, try to find relief or meaning
in the illusionary patterns of my bedroom ceiling

I'd never tell - you can probably tell anyways
I hope my absence breaks down
all your fortresses and walls
and you knock on my door one afternoon
tell me "all my strength came from you"
and you grab my hands and then my face
ask for forgiveness and permission
I'd kiss your sad mouth
into a smile before you even got the words out

scorpio szn

I'd belong to you if you wanted
have been holding this torch out
waiting for you to grab it

sometimes other people want it
but they know that it's your mouth
I'm aching for - it's tragic

so I'll walk five thousand steps
five times a day
blowing out my eardrums
so I can't hear myself say

"there are better methods out there
for falling out of love than holding my heart
using it as a stress ball hoping I'll take your hint
to do the work or suffer"

little did you know I'll suffer either way
but I like how your hands feel on me

maybe if I walk enough
become as visibly ill as I feel
you'll say sorry for what I'm doing to my body
cause you've been here too

you've outgrown your pain
your hand-me-down heartbreak
you still want it to exist
you just don't want to feel it

you think I'm not going to be able to find
someone else who'd split a milk dud with me,
or happily accept some head in a movie theatre?
I know you think I'm smarter than you
but no one is that dumb or delusional

is any of the motivation to remain secure in
my affections to delay closure
am I simply an enemy of the state you're in
and you're supposed to keep me closer

exhausted beyond the point of picking a new
fight
a "trying to get over me" neophyte
it can't be unobvious - the puddle I melt into
when our mutual gaze isn't abruptly
extinguished
you tell me freely you hate that I love you
and I agree but you'd only just wished for this

post-mortem curiosity

I've always been the one to say:
"you don't need to tell on yourself so loudly"
but I'd be bereft and so insincere
to not thank you for your social modesty
shame isn't a qualifier
but one's idiosyncratic nature and habits
aren't for everyone to indulge
so allow me to divulge -
am I worth the time and effort
to think about at all?
to crack jokes and one-liners so casually
or spew venom to anyone who'll listen?
I've given you plenty of ammunition to
accost and hold me hostage
but maybe you take pity and spare me
and my existence from your memory

oh so quiet... shhh..shhh..

I miss you in such a quiet way
the do not disturb, phone silenced kind of
typing-things-I-think-you'd-have-liked-to-hear-
(maybe this time last year)-quietly

walking along winding paths lined with trees
headphones left at home
leaves lovingly strewn by nature's flower girl
not one left alone
blowing hair out of faces and red into cheeks
bright orange, golden scarlets muddled into
burnt copper, ochred maroons dulling as
the sun rests much earlier these eves
kind of quietly

deep breaths released, genuine smiles, relieved
to be in the season of decay
that has never managed to smell sweeter
I'll keep it to myself - unless
I see you in the odd dream
and whisper to the wind that brings me peace
when I actually leave my house
on my pedestrian-friendly street
praying that it's never really your face I see

kind

of

quietly

ugly duckling

I am a sitting duck you happily toss
fiberglass breadcrumbs
I chew on them til my gums bleed
episodic filler for the plot
you wouldn't ask if you didn't need me
to tell you things that you could Google
my friends tell me I'm being used, I'll
just nod and agree

not going to argue
or try to convince you I'm worth it
I either am, or I'm not and you'll figure it out
but in the meantime
you'll text when you're bored and I,
knowing *I* am the object of your affections,
will smile with only my lips to hide
my bloodstained, perfectly straight dentition

I don't love you any less
so why would I stop trying to impress you
with just how patient I can be
I'd wait eternally
and keep chewing until you stop feeding me

benchmark

same house, same car,
same love in my heart
newer job, fewer calls,
fresh cuts and raw scars
still sting, can't let my touch linger

similar routine
I'm sure there've been tweaks
fancy degree on my wall finally

still laugh at old jokes,
still have your old clothes
I said I'd never wear them

I guess we both
have promises we broke

I still look at the moon
like you hung her
still feel your lips
like mine belong there

and you show up at my place
on our what-could've-been dates
I'm too excited to see you to think

coincidences like this can't exist

I flip through the photos
watching my smile
fade and grow
I've written for days about you
still holding onto the ache just in case
I ever get to meet the real you

que sera sera

a directionless outflux of love and admiration
myriads of stories I tell your stratus apparition
wherever I see her, though I'd much prefer
face to face, holding your hand
hearing your voice and your laugh

so much has happened in the past six months
and yet if you were here to ask, in nonchalance
I'd struggle to find an event to mention
that I didn't wish had gone differently
no matter how proud you told me you were of
me

I like to think you'd read these and feel seen
but that thought is just as heartwrenching as it is
comforting

the linearity of grief is nonexistent
but I hope the place all my love for you goes
isn't

ride or die

to be known is to be loved
what happens when no one wants to know me?
I'm in too deep to feel this green

Irvin Yalom spoke of multiple deaths
once when your heart stops, the next
- the last time you are thought of
it's meant to happen linearly
but timing's never been my forte

I exist to entertain, my tapestry
of stories woven into theatre
but a person can only watch so many tragedies
so, I'll aspire to be a good cheerleader
stand off to the side, out of the way
of actual success
the healthcare heroes and dream chasers
to my teacher's pets

people drift apart for fewer reasons than I've
handed out
I've moved too far, too frequently
for men with whom I no longer speak
under the guise of chasing imposter dreams

I disrupt forged rituals and routines
my pity party tantrums are incendiary
and could light all the birthday candles that
won't be blown out
when life gets too busy
when I'm no longer kitschy
enough to be worth traveling to see

if I could be the right kind of clever
I'd fashion a button or some sort of lever
for every person I've ever known and cherished
to let the love I have for them linger, illuminate
dark moments
have the rest of myself wiped from their
existence

my mediocrity is measurable
I will one day cease to be memorable
and it will be better for all
hearts that I had a hand in breaking
and ears that endured endless complaining

I fear they're too good for my world
the guilt would force their hand to falter
fixed in coin-toss odds
of whether I'm right or not
if they'd be better off

no evidence has come to light, no damning
receipts revealed
in the collective lives we've shared to make me
feel
any less than irreplaceable
but what happens in two years? in twenty?
eventually there won't be room for me
when my bridesmaid dresses become dusty
souvenirs, postcard reminders
that the people I love most
have someone else who loves them more
and I'm left alone in a room of funhouse mirrors
staring at the common denominator

www.ingramcontent.com/pod-product-compliance
Lightning Source LLC
LaVergne TN
LVHW041244200726
843507LV00013B/2813